Limericks, Philosophical & Literary

Limericks, Philosophical & Literary

Justin Clemens

Surpllus

'Now swarme many versifiers that neede never auswere to the name of Poets.'
—Sir Philip Sidney

Contents

Dedication and Author's Note

I would like to dedicate this collection to
friends who are also friends of the limerick.
First, to Joeri Mol, who first suggested that it
might be comical to turn philosophical
discourses, such as Benedict Spinoza's *Ethics*,
into limericks. Next, to Joseph Hughes and Jon
Rubin, whose own limerickings of propositions
and demonstrations from the aforementioned
Ethics are amazing. Third, to Janice Richardson,
who allegedly spontaneously snorted upon
hearing one of the limericks reproduced here,
which I took, perhaps illegitimately, as a kind of
endorsement. Fourth, to Sophy Williams, who,
besides being the only person acknowledged
here whose first name does not being with a 'J',
has claimed that two of the following limericks
—if only two!—are pretty good indeed.

The committed reader will find an
'Afterword' to this book which sets out a few
facts and opinions about the limerick form in
general, and about these limericks in particular.

Since the present limerickal catalogue of
my intellectual heroes is, if preponderantly
canonical, also to a certain extent idiosyncratic,
I have provided brief notes to the lives and times
of the subjects at the back of the book. I cannot
however vouch for the even-handedness or
veracity of these accounts.

Preface

Dear Reader, these limericks were writ
In unconscionable spasm of wit:
    For reasons unsure
    They burst through the door
Of consciousness—where they don't fit.

I

There once was a poet named Mallarmé,
An aesthete who couldn't obey
 Demands of his purse,
 But—*quant à* pure verse—
Could write for a year and a day.

There once was a wrestler named Plato
Who found that his verses turned sago:
   In rage and disgust
   He called them a bust
And stormed off to play with his Phaedo.

III

Old Socrates was a stonemason
Who found himself constantly chasin'
    Young men with ideas
    They couldn't keep clears—
Their heads didn't have enough space in.

I once heard a strange tale of Tom
Aquinas, that overweight dom,
    That he, as a trick,
    Had coined the limerick,
Between his discourses on Sodom.

V

There was an old sage known as Laozi
Who puzzled what could and could not be,
   When he realised the Way
    Was not easy to say—
For it is and is not entropy.

In a small room a lady named Emily
Ensconced herself so as to see
 If nobbled repose
 Would help her compose
The black milk of pure poetry.

VII

There was a young Jew called Spinoza
Whose ethics were those of a *poseur*.
    Considering God
    He proposed something odd—
That He was no more than *Natura*.

There was a French thinker Foucault,
Who went where no others would go,
   To torture and sex
   And knowledge's hex
In forging our penal a-go-go.

There was a young woman called Mary,
Whose preferences were for the scary;
On one stormy night
She sat down to write
Dr Frankenstein's composite faery.

An Austrian named Sigmund Freud
Found he became properly employed
    The moment he tasked
    His patients unmasked
To speak of the work of the void.

An ancient Greek sage who believed
In lessening all he might need,
    Soon found it was meet
    To wank in the street—
But it wouldn't provide a good feed.

A likely young fellow named Frank
Was eager for much higher rank:
    After years of snide fakin'
    They made him Lord Bacon—
Though his enterprise still kind of stank.

XIII

A promising cricketer, Beckett,
Told Oirish friends they could go feck it:
    He was moving to Paris
    To try to embarrass
The theatre—if not to wreck it.

Young Jeremy Bentham once saw
To modify people, the law
    Could better effect
    Travails of respect
Panopticalising the poor.

One night in a stove Descartes dreamt
Existence was somewhat exempt
   From claims of extension,
    Which held for distension—
But not for the wholly dirempt.

There once was a Lady Murasaki,
Who became not unreasonably snarky,
    For to live in a palace
    Is a poisonous chalice—
As she so described in her *Genji*.

If men are oft bloated with pride,
No wonder that girls become snide—
    For pure prejudice
    Is hot as undress,
As Austen so finely descried.

A clever young blighter named Zeno
(Who doesn't appear in the *Meno*)
    Thought Achilles got beat
    By a turtle in heat—
But better than gambling in Reno.

XIX

In Nishapur, Omar Khayyam,
While mashing the cubics to jam,
    Decided he might
    For sake of delight
Try poems in lieu of the spam.

An Algerian, name of Camus,
Was convinced of no reason to do:
    Whether loving the summer
    Or interring your mumma,
It's absurd anyway, boo-hoo-hoo.

There once was a scholar named Kong
Whose beard grew so frightfully long,
    Whenever he spoke,
    It coiled like pale smoke,
As if he'd been chugging a bong.

A fellow named Aimé Césaire
Was driven to rage and despair,
    For the colonised state
    Should have met a quick fate,
But somehow hung round like foul air.

A woman whose name was Beauvoir
Would sit, drink and smoke in the bar:
    But once on a bender
    She realised her gender
Just wasn't a luxury car.

XXIV

An impossible woman called Weil
Believed distance and suffering the Way
    We're sure of God's love,
    For He, from above,
Sent his only son *mortuus dei*.

A young man named Évariste Galois
Was destined to be a maths star
    But his radical ways
    And a woman's loose stays
Saw group theory stunned by a bar.

A hairy old fellow named Marx
Liked getting well drunk in town parks;
    One day he exclaimed,
     'God, labour's been maimed
By teeth of the capitalist sharks!'

A puritan known as John Milton
Made poetry something like Stilton:
    Rich, waxy and white
    With substance and bite,
To be served in the pub and the Hilton.

A maths guy whose surname was Grothendieck
Was proven a horrible freak:
    When problems were found
    He'd sit on the ground
And have them all solved in a week.

There was a young shrink, Frantz Fanon,
Made sick by unjust goings-on,
    Who showed some persistence
    In leading resistance,
Though hounded by cop and by don.

An odd German, name of George Cantor,
Was famed for his wit and his banter:
    You can take, he would say,
    The transfinite away,
But still there's enough to decanter!

And lest we forget Georges Bataille,
He wrote the rude *Tale of the Eye*—
    A story for trippers
    And anarchs in slippers,
That strange angry man Georges Bataille.

A reactionary fellow was Mishima,
Who had many grave issues with Papa,
   He loved to work out,
    Get out and about—
But maybe he took it too... far?

A dreamy young medic named Keats,
Seduced by the race of the beats
   Of Shakespeherean sonnets
   And gods in old bonnets,
Would dance them in pantomime cleats.

A German Jew, Hannah Arendt,
Who was of most serious bent,
    Found much of her life
    Caught up in the strife
Where meaningful meanings are meant.

XXXV

There once was a poet-cum-lawyer
Who hardly left his office foyer.
    When colleagues asked, 'Wallace,
    'How do you find solace?'
He said, 'Well, I'm kind of a Boyar.'

XXXVI

There was a great Dane, Kierkegaard,*
Who might well have been a glum bore,
    But his plays with false names
    And other such games
Made him a star turn on the floor.

* To be pronounced in the Danish fashion.

XXXVII

An ill-tempered thinker named Popper
Once looked like becoming a cropper—
    Through cunning and chance,
    He swung the romance,
And turned out to be a show stopper.

There once was a snob Tanizaki,
Who rejected the lame and the lackey;
    He called out the West
    For tainting the best,
And Enlightenment for being tacky.

XXXIX

A writer named J.L. Borges
Said anything somebody says
   Is something that nothing
   Can void into stuffing
For anyone not in high-res.

A toffee-nosed woman named Woolf
Was wise to the warp and the woof;
   She held women needed
   To be less impeded
By lack of an income and roof.

An Indigenous activist who
Was sick of colonial flu,
   Decided her name
   Was part of the same—
So she changed it to Oodgeroo.

A famous bushranger and debtor
Dictated a furious letter:
    You cops are all c-ts,
    Your laws cunning stunts,
By G-d you should all do much better!

There once was a woman named George
Who turned her home desk to a forge:
    She pumped out great novels
    Of houses and hovels
While staring out over life's gorge.

There was a young rake called John Donne—
A veritable canon of fun—
    But he was unmade
    By marrying in shade,
And ended a patron of dun.

LXV

A classical scholar named Doolittle
Was customed to chip and to whittle,
    Until her tight verse
    Was perfectly terse—
And its end found a fang in the *Mittel*.

A philosopher known as Val Plumwood,
Considered the *must* and the *should*,
    When a croc one fine day
    Tried to make her his prey —
She knew what it was to be food.

LVII

There was a Parisian, Villon—
Montcorbier, Loges, or Mouton—
    For he was, as you see,
    On a criminal spree
And often confounded his *noms*.

A writer named Zora Neale Hurston
From Eatonville rose just to burst on
    The scene with her work
    Which never did shirk
The requirements of representation.

XLIX

A blushing Romantic, Leopardi,
Was someone you'd want at your party:
    Depressive and weak,
    A natural-born geek,
Yet handsome, well-apportioned, and arty.

Parmenides thought hard about ones
That never are manys or nones:
    His rigour was such
    It turned Double-Dutch
And Being ran away with his puns.

There once was a scholar Du Fu,
Who wished for what all scholars do,
    But the moon of events
    Swelled the tide-waves of sense
And flushed his career down the loo.

A woman named Wollstonecraft found
The numbers of bounders abound,
   So she set to compose
   A great treatise in prose
Where rights of all women resound!

LIII

Rossetti once wrote of dispute
Of sisters, a market, and fruit
  Purveyed by the goblins
  To suck the young girls in—
The whole thing was really a hoot.

There once was a sage, Nagarjuna,
Who proffered a paradox lunar:
    For something to be,
    It's nothing, you see—
Yet this inexistence'll ruin 'ya.

There was a young fellow called Saul
Whose fervour could sometimes appal,
   Then he fell off his ass
   With a crashing of brass,
And got up again as St Paul.

A monsieur named Gustave Flaubert
Had wonderful absence of hair,
   He used his bald spot
   To beat dash and dot
To tunes for a slow dancing bear.

LVII

For once a good woman named Gwen,
Unmatched for the wit of her pen,
    Carved, crossed by some ticks
    Keaching blood, acrostics
Deep into the vertical's Sten.

LVIII

A writer of fictions, Le Guin,
Showed evil, through thick and through thin,
   Would never stop chasing—
   And no self-abasing
Would save her young hero from sin.

A ruddy young Englishman, Blake,
Was found to be dreaming awake:
    When asked what he'd seen
    He rubbed his eyes clean,
And spoke of God pashing a Snake.

A shrink, name of Melanie Klein,
Could turn any *Ja* into *Nein*:
    She didn't believe
    In innocent Eve,
Nor claim that young Dawn would be fine.

A logic professor called Hegel
Acquired the form of a bagel,
   Through radical thought
   Embodied the nought
With dough from Kant, Fichte and Schlegel.

A woman named Judith A. Wright
Was seized by the nature of site,
    Of birds and of drought,
    Of cruelty and doubt,
And love that inspires you to flight.

A dubious fellow called Legman
Inspired the current collection—
    His hot-takes on jokes,
    On smut and on smokes,
Pervert the received intellection.

A poet named W. B. Yeats
Lived many alternative states:
   His poems of Oisin,
   Cuchulain and Cathleen,
Are really incredibly greats.

There was a great wit, Oscar Wilde,
Whom Merry Olde England beguiled,
   But made the mistake
   Of poking a snake...
Which ended with charges being filed.

Our singular Clarice Lispector
Dissected the ghoul and the spectre,
   In coiled monologues
   Embroiled monstrous fogs
Of creatures like lictor and lector.

A maths genius called Emmy Noether
(In physics much greater than Goethe),
    Would conjure ideals
    From rings without seals:
The symmetries didn't desert her.

A short man named Thomas de Quincey
Who loved the outrageous and chintzy,
   Got madly addicted
   To opium liquid
Then wrote till his brains went all tintzy.

A rigorous fellow, Herr Kant,*
Was really a bit of a grunt:
    When Königsberg wives
    Used him in their lives
For timing it wasn't a stunt.

* To be pronounced in the German manner.

That cultist Pythagoras thought
Reality was never nought,
    And squares of the sides
    Were fine to divides—
As long as root 2 wasn't taught.

A mathematician, Hypatia,
Who researched Plotinian Nature,
    Found she'd run afoul
    Of mitre and cowl,
Becoming a martyr of stature.

A philologist named Erich Auerbach
Fled the Nazis without his book stack;
    Yet base deprivations
    In refugee stations
Somehow did not make him a hack.

There once was a dude Heraclitus
Who suffered from human detritus:
   In horror at what
   We'd made of our lot,
He died in some cowshit to spite us.

There once was a person called Proust
Who ruled the fashionable roost,
    But gave it away
    In order to lay
Out memories both juicy and *juste*.

LXXV

A poet and painter called Loy
Was hardly retiring or coy:
    She wrote out her life
    In turmoil and strife
Which mixed up the shame with the joy.

There once was a god given lass
Who altered her name to Duras.
    She wrote *Lol. V. Stein*
    While slamming down wine—
But thinking of bombs and of gas.

LXXVII

A woman named Marianne Moore
(A presbyter lover of law)
 Wrote of her dislike
 Of poetry's shrike
That lessens the more it is more.

Postface

These limericks—which deal with the dead—
End too in that bottomless bed
   But if you're alive
   Do dream as you dive
With ghosts yet undone though well-said.

Afterword

'Under the mask of humour, all men are enemies.'
—Gershon Legman

This is a book of limericks. The subjects are famous thinkers, philosophical and literary.

The limerick is a humble and common verse form. It is also emblematically, if not exclusively, *English*.

The limerick is also a relatively recent development. As Cyril Bibby, the educator and eminent historian of science, writes: 'the earliest known publications consisting exclusively of limericks, in quite recognisably modern form, appeared in London between 1820 and 1823'.[1] One of these early publications —*The History of Sixteen Wonderful Old Women*—contains, for example, the following:

> There was an Old Woman named Towl,
> Who went out to Sea with her Owl,
>   But the Owl was Sea-sick,
>   And scream'd for Physic;
> Which sadly annoy'd Mistress Towl.[2]

If it fully emerges in the nineteenth century —although its precursors reach back much further—the limerick's decisive moment came with Edward Lear, undisputed master of and proselytiser for the genre in Victorian England. After the success of his *A Book of Nonsense*, first published under the pseudonym 'Derry down Derry' in 1846, but only really becoming popular on its republication over subsequent decades (the expanded 1861 re-edition was the first on which Lear's name appeared as such), the limerick spread like wildfire across the whole of the English-speaking world.[3] Limericks, interestingly, did not receive their canonical name until sometime in the 1880s. Why and how they came to be called 'limericks' at all is still a matter of conjecture. Although sometimes identified with the Irish town or county of Limerick, this attribution is—as is so often the case with limericks—highly uncertain.[4]

The limerick's powers are modest. It is a part of 'light' or 'nonsense' literature, being too brief, too silly, too formalised to ever really achieve the seriousness and substantiality of higher kinds, even when, as is surprisingly often the case, limericks take art, religion, philosophy, politics or ethics as their topics. Short and jaunty, not-entirely-funny and mildly shameless, a limerick typically elicits indecent little psychophysical twitches in response: smirks and groans and baas.

Yet the limerick, much like its other vulgar relatives, thereby poses a problem for criticism. What makes for a good limerick, for example? Popularity? Longevity? Variability? Silliness? Could a 'good limerick'—even assuming the existence of such—ever be said to be a 'good poem'? As Wim Tigges notes, it is an open question as to 'whether such a slight thing as the limerick, so often indeed associated with obscene doggerel, can under any conditions be said to have an aesthetic value'.[5] Doggerel or not, limericks continue to circulate throughout the English-speaking world today, sustained by an abiding if enigmatic popular fascination.

The history of limericks is indissociable from comic magazines such as *Punch*, from occasional anthologies, from newspaper competitions, from gift annuals and samizdat publications of all kinds. In print, it is remarkable how often the verbal quirks of the limerick are accompanied and extended by satirical sketches and cartoons. As Quentin Blake remarks of Lear's own publications, which famously mix word and image: 'the nonsense drawings and their verses go so well and naturally together that hardly anybody has felt the necessity of commenting on it'.[6] In Blake's view, the verbal scenarios provide inspirational material for the illustrator, working in Lear's case as a kind of double machine of sound and vision. Blake's point is a good one: what does come first for Lear, the limerick or cartoon?

Limericks are very often anonymous. Aside from Lear himself, the most famous names in the world of limericks tend not to be the authors but the anthologists, eminent enthusiasts such as Bennett Cerf (one of the founders of Random House), Gershon Legman (one of the strangest and most significant folklorists of the twentieth century), and Carolyn Wells (the successful writer and anthologist of crime fictions). However, it must also immediately be added that, where limericks are concerned, the line between author and anthologist is notably porous, as is the line between collector and disseminator. One can never be quite certain whether an anthologist has slyly slipped one or two compositions of his or her own into the mix.

Here, for instance, is one either written or reproduced by the incomparably rebarbative Norman Douglas, scandalous bon vivant, elegant author of the Mediterranean classic *South Wind*, and bête noir of D.H. Lawrence:

There was a young woman of Twickenham
Who regretted that men had no prick in 'em.
   On her knees every day
   To God she would pray
To lengthen and strengthen and thicken 'em.[7]

And here is an altogether cleaner, uncredited variation by Bennett Cerf, which, it has to be said, nonetheless retains a not-altogether-attenuated link to its precursor:

There was a young woman of Twickenham
Loved sausages—never got sick on 'em.
   She knelt on the sod
   And prayed to her God
To lengthen and strengthen and thicken 'em.[8]

The limerick is relatively simple to define, if —as ever—complexities rapidly emerge. The paradigmatic limerick is a five-line verse, rhyming *aabba*, in which there are three stresses in the *a* lines, two in the *b* lines. Although the limerick stanza has occasionally been displayed as a four-liner, the *bb* lines printed as one —Lear's own work being a case in point—it is above all the five-liner that has swept the field. One presumes this is due to the odd asymmetry of the prime, given that all the familiar rhyming stanzaic forms in English (and many other European languages) are couplets, quatrains, octets, sonnets, and so on, which are of course divisible by two. In such circumstances, a five-line verse presents as an incompetent quatrain —a deliberate and patent incompetence essential to the charm of the form.

The limerick metre is usually anapaestic, consisting of two unstressed syllables followed by one stressed syllable. Almost all accounts of the form also note that, due to catalexis—the dropping of a syllable from the start of a line —the rhythm easily becomes amphibrachic, unstressed-stressed-unstressed.[9] The usual patterns of English enunciation are deformed in limericks, where an emphasis often has to be put on a word due to its placement that would be clumsy or mistaken in ordinary intercourse. The reader will meet with a number of examples of the familiar variations in the course of this book. As Bibby remarks, 'each language has its own metrical quality, and that of English lies in stress and rhythm rather than in syllabic length. It is so rich in consonants that we have learned to make light work of them, sometimes even slurring them almost to the point of extinction.'[10] Bibby demonstrates metrical variations of the limerick that are quite staggering, and he ends his illuminating technical investigations with a brilliant little limerick on the very subject:

> There was a young Scot named McAmiter,
> Who bragged of excessive diameter;
> Yet it wasn't the size
> That opened their eyes,
> But the rhythm—trochaic hexameter.

This free metrical variation of limericks should not hinder us from emphasising that the anapaest is the precise reverse of the dactyl (stressed-unstressed-unstressed). As dactylic hexameter was the spine of the great ancient epics of Homer and Vergil, the limerick's vacillating anapaestic inversions evince an anti-epical animus. Limericks are so anti-epical, in fact, that they often can't even sustain the courage—or the cowardice—of their own formal convictions.

A limerick's content is usually rude, nonsensical or perverse, if—precisely because of its formal constraints—it also tends towards the conservative edge of such phenomena. Its characteristic obscenities are, for the most part, not avant-gardist or experimental, no matter how much they might seem to contravene good taste or common morality. The general concerns of the limerick are those of nonsense literature more generally: eating and being eaten, fucking and being fucked, hating and humiliating, mayhem, mutilation, murder, and metamorphosis.

It is noteworthy how often—despite two hundred years of public experimentation on a planetary scale—the first (and sometimes even the last) lines of limericks tend to revert to the limited locutions already canonical with Lear. Such lines begin 'There was…' or 'There once was', immediately introducing a personage, specified by age or sex, as coming from this or that place, e.g., 'There was an old man of Tobago', 'There was a young lady of Riga', 'There was a small boy of Quebec'. Indeed, as W.S. Baring-Gould, the celebrated author of the first 'biography' of the fictional detective Sherlock Holmes, has itemised, certain places, for one reason or another—euphony, rivalry, ridiculousness—have become recurrent *topoi* for limerickal inventiveness. The town of Crewe is one of these; Calcutta is another.[11] As one limerick itself puts it:

> Throughout the whole world, experts say
> That it's GEOGRAPHY RULES! O.K.?
>   Though it's not the location
>   But the mere appellation
> That's important down Limerick way.

Alternatively, we find a person specified by nation or location, whose name is often ludicrous yet stereotypical, and primed for the (ridiculous) rhymes to follow: MacTrigger, Pitt, Mapes, Primmet, and so on. Both formats are reduced enough to be formalisable by the most basic grammatical categories, e.g., [There was: (indef art.): (adjective): (person): (preposition): (toponym)]. These are of course not the only popular structures for the limerick, the flyting of real, particular enemies, named, blamed and shamed—a version beloved by James Joyce and other *litterateurs*—being another notable possibility. This third variation naturally tends also to be the most varied in its content, as it is usually calibrated to some peculiar feature, detail or act of the personage in question.

There are also the rare successes in which the form takes itself as its own object. Let me give two famous instances of the latter. First:

The limerick packs laughs anatomical
Into space that is quite economical.
But the good ones I've seen
So seldom are clean,
And the clean ones so seldom are comical!

Second, a W.S. Gilbert parody of a Lear original:

There was a young man of St. Bees
Who was stung in the arm by a wasp;
When they said, 'Does it hurt?',
He replied, 'No it doesn't;
It's a good job it wasn't a hornet!'

Along with such formal reflexions, the afore-mentioned triumvirate of variations—there was an *x* of *y*, there was an *x* called *y*, and the third naming the *gestes et opinions* of real persons—seems almost to exhaust the genre of limericks in its entirety.

The extraordinarily conservative insistence of such base syntagms should alert us to some implications that, in their very simplicity, repetitiveness and pervasiveness, too often go unremarked. Take, first and foremost, the *there was*: the indeterminate historic past conjured up by this phrase not only at once informs us that we are in the ambit of fairy tales and historical anecdotage, but also implies that the coming subject of the tale may well (have) come to a sticky end. Indeed, the sorry fate of many limerickal subjects is presumably so well known as not to require further harping-upon. Yet it is worth lingering upon the canonical tense of the limerick. *There was*, it asserts—as it implies, *but no longer*. As the German philosopher Martin Heidegger says of *Dasein* (broadly speaking, human existence), *there is only a was*. The point is not that *Dasein* has simply passed away, because something would first have to have been present in order to be past, but that this character only-ever-emerges-as-always-already-gone. The characters presented by such limericks are never *present* as such, although the *place* from which they hail, however minor, certainly lingers. The constitutive nostalgia, the cruel melancholy of limericks, is patent from the very first. To parody the critic Walter Benjamin, death is the sanction of everything the limerick can tell. Every limerick is a mocking and fragmentary emissary of oblivion, of the vital obsolescence of all human endeavours —not least itself. And yet, the very imperfection of the expression *there was* is not preteritic, but potentially progressive. The gone may well have gone—but it has not entirely went.

Second, the prevalence of the indefinite article is linked in this subgenre to the suppression of proper names, that is, the preeminent markers by which humans recognise humans *as* humans, and which often function for ordinary folk and philosophers as the linguistic paradigm of personal identity. But it is not so much a dehumanisation that is at stake in this limerickal suppression of nomination, as a kind of cruel play with the generic markers of humankind itself. In the alternative subgenres that provide usually clearly false or exaggerated proper names, these names suggest a satirical catalogue of stereotypes. This impression is, third, further reinforced by the abstract adjectives such as 'old', 'young', 'odd', and so forth, that modify, fourth, the otherwise vacant 'men', 'women', 'girls', and 'boys' that populate such limericks. The nouns bespeak—if anything —a kind of utterly basic human dimorphic biology, with the expectation, of course, that they will turn out in this case *not to be proper at all*. Indeed, both common nouns and proper names are hijacked by the limerick in order to evacuate them of their properness, their properties, and their proprieties. The limerick is a machine for anthropological depropriation. Finally, fifth, the line tends to end with the invocation of a toponym, a little-known locality in your own country or colony, a name which, for the most part, will not bring with it any particular detail or require any particular knowledge, other than signifying its own irrelevance, vacuity, or outlandishness. Commentators have sometimes opined that this obsession with toponyms and provenance that utterly dominates the genre is itself tied to the geographical and historical curricula of English school rooms. A limerick proffers a parodic mimicry of learning.

No wonder that the limerick is, in its pedagogical aspect, considered appropriate for children, as, in its populist aspect, presumed to appeal to vulgar, depraved, or otherwise immature personages. This has historically been the fate of the form, flanked by harmless nonsense on the one side, and ineffectual obscenity on the other. Yet, as Norman Douglas once wrote: 'Saints are dead—they have died out from sheer inability to propagate their species; limericks are alive, and their procreative capacity is amazing'.[12] One reason that limericks procreate so impressively is undoubtedly due to their constitutional lack of saintliness. Sandwiched between the infantile and the perverse, the limerick is a little incitation to regress, to aggress, and to egress—before quickly scurrying back to the fold of normality again.

Almost all limericks tend to tell a little story, in which the final line offers a payoff or punchline of some kind. If I have already noted the limerick's affiliations with mass schooling and with popular print, there is no doubt that the limerick is also a little bit obituary, a little bit *fait divers*—perhaps even a little bit shonky advertising—thoroughly parasitic on the minor components of the print media of modern times. As a mockery of the news item and the death notice, the limerick functions as a fantasy counter-memorial. A feeling of life can sometimes only come from a little burst of comic death. For his part, Baring-Gould quotes Morris Bishop quoting an unnamed 'scholarly writer' in the *Times Literary Supplement*: 'the form is essentially liturgical, corresponding to the underlying ritual of Greek tragedy, with the *parodos* of the first line, the *peripeteia* of the second, the *stichomythia* of the two short lines... and the *epiphaneia* in the last'.[13] The limerick's utterly fixed allusive—and elusive—mutability can clearly inspire a disorderly classicism amongst its aficionados.

Like jokes, limericks circulate not only in print, but also orally. Constantly travelling between orality and print, playing the line between what can't and what shouldn't be said, limericks are the late and toothless scions of the notorious early modern libels and lampoons, which swarmed about persons and offices much

to the perturbation of such legal minds as
Francis Bacon and Edward Coke.[14] Due to their
brevity, lively metre, simple rhyming, and
risqué content, limericks are like mnemonic
Velcro, exceptionally easy to remember and
recite.

And, also much like jokes — at least
according to Sigmund Freud — limericks
thereby engage the repressed laws of the tribe,
simultaneously expressing the contingent,
nonsensical and obscene nature of all such
repressions, while once more occluding and
reaffirming them. Social taboos and personal
anxieties are exposed and disseminated, but
also carefully masked and leashed by the
limerick. Hence each limerick is also a disavowed autobiography of its compositor or
disseminator. This signature happens at the
level of form, as much as of content. All major
critics of the form stress the operational signifi-
cance of the limerick's typical misprisions.
The misspellings and mispronunciations, the
misattributions, misstatements and flat-out
mistakes constitute little festive moments of
linguistic aggression.[15] As the French philosopher Gilles Deleuze might have put it, limericks suggest that the logic of sense is itself
nonsense.[16]

Yet these misprisions are, as I have said,
oddly conservative. Norman Douglas himself
underlines the imperialist affiliations of the
limerick, if with a certain satirical flair. His
tongue-in-cheek remarks touch on something

uncomfortable or discomforting about the politics of forms. Not every marginal form has been 'marginalised' because it is somehow a threat to the dominant orders of the day; sometimes, the apparent marginality is covertly in the service of the orders to which it may seem to constitute an exception or rebuke. To simply reassert the rights of this or that form against its undue 'marginalisation', 'suppression' or even 'erasure' is not only to misunderstand the complex ecologies of symbolic form, but risk inadvertently or unconsciously reaffirming the very powers one claims to be fighting against. Some forms do indeed break with normality as an assault against established powers; others do so precisely in order to limn and affirm the precedence of the norms with which they break. I believe the limerick is of this latter kind. Despite its flagrant rejection of epic qualities in and for itself, the limerick remains an unconfessed accomplice of the imperial epic.

By the same token, it is also misleading to condemn *in toto* a form or motif for fulfilling —or failing to fulfil—this or that function at this or that moment. For a start, one should ask whether such a use expresses an essential bond, and not merely an accidental or occasional relationship. In any case, forms are in principle aesthetically irreducible to any particular political position. Perhaps they are even more difficult, contradictory, and paradoxical than this. Douglas has wittily noted that the limerick is 'historically speaking... a protest against protestantism, and strange to think that our little ones would never have learnt to babble about "the old man of Kent, whose tool was remarkably bent", or the "young man of Fife, who couldn't get into his wife", but for Luther's preaching and the victories of Naseby and Dunbar'. If Douglas' satirical account is to be credited, the limerick is an emblematically, constitutionally English nationalist and post-religious form that develops as part of the English people's social and political emergence from Protestantism.

The limerick also seems to be an exceptionally masculinist genre, as its commentators note. Even accounting for the form's integral relation with anonymity, there are surprisingly few women associated with the limerick, even though the subjects of limericks are perhaps disproportionately female. In Legman's words: 'Women do not often like bawdy limericks, in which they generally figure as both villain and victim'.[17] Perhaps then the ambitions of the limerick are near-invariably masculinist, nationalist, and imperialist at best—or flat-out misogynist, racist and imperialist at worst. But there are further possibilities. After all, the limerick's cornball energies can seem to gesture towards revolution and imperium at once. The past of the limerick is post-Protestant protestation; its present, the real of colonial domination. And its future? We will see. Whatever the case, limericks undeniably speak to and of the *corniness* of the imperial subject: each one simultaneously notable and nugatory, singular and standardised.

If the form is indeed publicly presented as a definitive guarantor of levity, nonsense and obscenity, it can be deployed to smuggle in real ambitions and profound feelings that would otherwise seem offensive, too difficult to treat, or mere folly. Take the British Prime Minister Clement Attlee's well-known autobiographical limerick, written in old age in a certain satisfaction with his own achievements:

Few thought he was even a starter
There were those who thought themselves
    smarter
But he ended PM
CH and OM
An earl and a knight of the garter.

Although Attlee's is hardly the most impressive instance of a celebrated person using the limerick for his or her own ends, it does suggest something further about the appeal of the limerick to an extraordinary range of persons famous for other matters. Well-known persons can holiday, as it were, in the slums of the limerick, while showing off their wit and versatility. Although I have noted the resolute anonymity of the great bulk of limericks, it is also the case that many great writers have tried their hands at the form, some of them perhaps rather surprising. Aside from writers such as Lewis Carroll or Ogden Nash, esteemed for their nonsense verse and therefore naturally also authors of celebrated limericks, we also find contributions by such luminaries as W. H. Auden, James Joyce, Rudyard Kipling, Christopher Logue, Gabriel Dante Rossetti, Salman Rushdie, and H. G. Wells. The list goes on and on.

Here is Dylan Thomas' celebrated riff on the virgin birth:

There was an old bugger called God,
Who got a young virgin in pod.
    This disgraceful behaviour
    Begot Christ our Saviour,
Who was nailed to a cross, poor old sod.

And, to complete the trinity, here is a final example from the great science-fiction writer Isaac Asimov, who—perhaps surprisingly to his millions of fans—was also a rabid aficionado of the limerick form, writing them in their thousands. Here is one, chosen almost at random (if with a certain local flavour that will not be lost on Antipodeans):

'We refuse', said two men from Australia,
'Bestiality this saturnalia.
    For now, we bethink us,
    The ornithorhynchus
Is our down-under type of Mammalia.'

Most of Asimov's limericks are obscene and lascivious, although he also wrote a large

111

number especially for children. Yet again, we find in all these instances the limerick's characteristic relation between the infantile and the perverse, the mocking and the canonical.

To invoke such professional or eminent authors as producers of limericks alerts us to one *desideratum* of form in the literary traditions of all times and all places. Not only to show one's range and skills, nor to enjoy a holiday from the serious, but also to extend and transform a form in the very use of the form, whether by using the form as a depository and vehicle for images and affects that it has previously resisted or been unable to bear, or by submitting its constraints to such pressure that they give way to something else, a something else that could not have been reached except through *that* form itself. Because forms, like all human endeavours, are volatile fragments and archives of historical antagonisms, they emerge and vanish in time—and therefore can be subjected to revaluating interventions. But perhaps such remarks are too abstract and general; after all, it is the *specificity* of the limerick that is at stake here.

I have noted that, however covertly tied to imperium it may be, the limerick tends to work by departing, however minimally or momentarily, from the official watchwords of that order by proffering a little precarious refuge from sense. The sense of this 'refuge from sense' is perhaps not as simple as one might imagine. As the French psychoanalyst Jacques Lacan remarks about jokes, this operation may be 'neither the absence of sense nor nonsense, but exactly the step that corresponds to a glimpse into what sense reveals about its own procedure'.[18] If we can perhaps consider every literary form as a momentary deadlock of competing expressive and repressive forces, it is also the case that the limerick offers itself as a form which exhibits its own tensions with a concentrated and extreme clarity. So even as the limerick casually promulgates the obscenities of the masters insofar as these are reuptaken by their subjects, it simultaneously offers a unique self-analysis of its own strategies.

Beyond the evidence of sexism, racism, and imperialism that limericks regularly flaunt in their flouting of social etiquette, there is —I have said it already—a very strong consensus among the critics of limericks of their integral tie to the English language itself. Even Legman, perhaps the most comparative of the collector-critics, can only really indicate rather loose analogues in Italian, French, Spanish, and Russian, rather than any plausible formal or material influences. As Bibby puts it, after citing a number of other commentators, 'the longer one studies limericks, the more strongly one is struck by their overwhelmingly strong affiliation with the English tongue'.[19] Perhaps we could put it even more strongly: *the limerick expresses the true genius of the English language in its imperial guise.*[20] Like a stamped and embossed coin of the realm, the unhinged deracinated repetitions of the limerick both presuppose and prove the formal essence of the modern imperial subject.

Yet, if it is indeed the case that the limerick expresses and exemplifies something essential to modern English, it is no surprise—in our era of globalisation and decolonial politics —that if the limerick remains at all popular today, it is as a *residual* form; perhaps even, we could say, a *zombie* form. For Legman, who believes that the modern nineteenth-century limerick was in fact already *only the ghost of the form*, which had been 'killed off' by being 'laundered out of existence' in the eighteenth century,[21] this would be a further outrage against the truth of the limerick's unbiddable obscenity.

In our own time, that of the internet, of trolls and tolls, of memes and machinima, the limerick still survives in some fashion or other —although it now clearly lacks the violent emergent energies of the new online forms or post-forms. As one wag put it on Twitter:

This thing that they call social media
Makes you needy—and then ever needier—
For the more that you do
The less that you're you
As your being becomes bickerpedia.

Tempting as it may be to suggest that the limerick has been one of the great *memes* of Anglophonic Empire, such anachronism is most likely inappropriate. Then again, it turns out that the ethologist Richard Dawkins, who coined the term 'meme' in his famous tract *The Selfish Gene*, had something just like a limerick in mind as the very paradigm of what he meant by a meme.[22] Indeed, as John Maynard Smith wrote in a review of another of Dawkins's books, *The Extended Phenotype*: 'A typical meme, as [Dawkins] then conceived it, is a limerick'.[23] The limerick is dead, long live the mimerick!

For the limerick has always flourished in its very inappropriateness, speaking mockingly of its subjects while forging a disavowed consensus of personal and political norms. It is as such a spectral zombie that I summon it here: a zombie form to speak ill of the living dead to the living dead. The form must bury the form for the living to shun and ignore, in a language at once omnipresent and decadent.

I have gently pushed here against what is usually considered to be the minimal and maximal ranges of the numbers of syllables in an acceptable limerick line. As long as these limericks can still be made, whether by accident or by force, to conform in most part to the exemplary stress patterns, I have been satisfied. I have also attempted to vary these stresses so that they range, from limerick to limerick, from the unconscionably jaunty to the leadenly serious. Part of the problem of rhyming foreign names is their very different pronunciations across the range of so-called 'World English', let alone in their original languages. What is to be

done with the Chinese and the Danes and the
French and the Germans and the Japanese?
I have mostly gone for an approximation of the
original language or sometimes just a parody
thereof. The rhymes suffer more and less from
such abusiveness.

Yet every one of the personalities repre-
sented in these limericks has been, at the very
least, a hero of sorts to me. As writers, thinkers,
scientists, and artists, they all struggled against
the usual ruck of forces that plague humanity.
Only a few enjoyed riches, reputation, and
power in their own lifetimes. Several came to
unfortunate and unpleasant endings. All are
now dead, if canonical in one way or another.
Although I know more about some than about
others, all have influenced and marked me
indelibly, and these limericks have been written
on the basis of memories of my encounters
with them. This means that *the opinions expressed*
by no means always follow the accepted, acceptable, or dominant genres of current reception
—not even my own. Sometimes, of course, they
do: Mary Shelley is present here as nothing but
the author of *Frankenstein*. Yet Villon, by con-
trast,—the greatest poet of mediaeval France
—is recalled only for his (almost forgotten)
pseudonyms. Moreover, as many of these
figures refuse the everyday divisions of labour
that so mark the deleterious experience of
terrestrial life, so these limericks necessarily
mark this refusal too.

Even in the compressed lines of a limerick,

I have tried to smuggle in something of the life and times, the character and tenor of these people, and there are many allusions, whether express or innate, to their singular contributions. These contributions are, by the same token, not always those that will inspire our current crop of violently moralising neo-Victorian hypocrites to enthusiasm. We know that Simone de Beauvoir, for instance, enjoyed a fag and a tipple; we know that George Eliot contravened the tenets of her age by living in sin with her paramour George Lewes; we know that François Villon and Ned Kelly were in fact outlaws, subsisting for the most part in penury and hunger, harried and pursued by the pitiless forces of law. All are once again traduced as they are apotheosised by their melancholical limerickeral memorialisations here.

Still, there cannot not be consequences of form. Since the limerick is one of the belittling forms par excellence, these verses praise through belittling, and belittle in their praise, the incomparable achievements of their subjects reduced to the ludicrous, the arbitrary, the irritating and the irrelevant. Moreover, these limericks are—and I can assert this with some authority given the thousands I have now read —rather too literary, learned, and lame compared to the outstanding exempla of the genre to compel any lasting attention. In fine, they perhaps constitute a kind of twee lit-crit, destined only too soon to join on the remainder table all those seasonal releases of light literary

117

litter that come and go: the shrinklits, the haiku rerenderings of classic tales, the cartoon and colouring-book extemporisations upon the canon.

In a word, these limericks present the form (mostly) emptied of its traditional *raisons d'être*—populism, nationalism, misogyny, vulgarity—, the old affects emptied of desire by the neutralisation of literary captivation in a sequence of questionable purposelessness. Still, in a world, our world, where the new conformity is not the obedient submission to norms or laws but the affirmation and exacerbation of 'disruption'—the quotidian political terrorism of psychopathic leaders and the economic terrorism of rapacious multinational corporations—then perhaps a true and viable contemporary nonconformity no longer involves such disruption. As Legman, perhaps the preeminent historian and anthologist of limericks, once remarked: 'meanwhile, perfectly lunatic fantasy sadism is shamelessly unleashed on an international scale in all the "media arts", as mass brainwashing for the genocides to come —when the food runs short'.[24] Against this 'lunatic fantasy sadism', then, we should perhaps envisage a nonconforming freedom for today indiscernible from the median and the mediocre, the insipid and banal. As with the fashion subculture of 'normcore', in which the nondescript and unremarkable become the keys to the kingdom, unperceived by power, recognisable, if at all, as 'just another x' of no especial interest, the middling *prêt-à-porter* becomes the work of true freedom. Or, to use a phrase by Heraclitus—the subject of limerick LXXIII here—*Limericks, Philosophical & Literary* proposes itself as a work of *palintropic harmony*, the untimely curving back of the ventral valve of the form upon itself.

After much fussing and pressing and confusion, these limericks have been reproduced in the strict order of their composition. As such, there are no geographical, formal, or chronological principles governing the sequence, other than those of accident, finitude (my own), and unconscious motivations. Why are there seventy-seven of them? Who knows?! How was it that I was unable to write limericks about other authors who have been at least as important to me? Angela Carter, Samuel R. Delany, Alexander Pushkin, Henry Miller, Sappho, Sylvia Plath, Richard Wright, and many others fail to grace these pages. And the preposterousness, irrelevance, and inelegance of these verses might certainly irritate, enervate, or repulse. I hope nevertheless that their essentially frivolous (if presently mortified) nature can, given the right light, eye, ear, and hand, still amuse and educate today.

Justin Clemens
Melbourne, 2019

Notes to the Afterword

1   C. Bibby, *The Art of the Limerick* (Stanmore: Cassell Australia, 1978), p. 42.

2   Anon., *The History of Sixteen Wonderful Old Women, Illustrated by as many Engravings; Exhibiting their Principal Eccentricities and Amusements* (London: Harris and Son, 1821). The first edition was 1820.

3   Lear's publications include *A Book of Nonsense* (1846), *Nonsense Songs, Stories, Botany and Alphabets* (1871), *More Nonsense Pictures, Rhymes, Botany, etc.* (1872), and *Nonsense Songs and Stories* (1895). It's worth underlining the pedagogical links of the limerick with alphabetisation and botanical information explicit in these titles.

4   This has hardly prevented the attempt being made, although the authorities either furiously disagree or agree that there can only be furious disagreement on this matter. In 2013, Matthew Potter published his inquiry *The Curious Story of the Limerick* (Limerick: The Limerick Writers' Centre, 2013), about which one should certainly note the publisher and the publisher's residence before fully endorsing his views. As Potter remarks: 'My own favourite theory is that the poetic form takes its name from the 18th century Maigue Poets, Seán Ó Tuama and Aindrias MacCraith, from Croom in Co Limerick who used it extensively in their works. They did not invent the limerick but probably gave their name to it, though in a roundabout way. The name arose in the late 1880s and early 1890s as a result of the efforts by W. B. Yeats and George Sigerson, leading figures in the Irish Literary Revival, to reclaim the limerick form from Edward Lear and to ascribe it instead to the Maigue Poets. This attracted the derision of the British literary establishment who began to use the term limerick for obscene versions', 'Is the limerick a Limerick invention?' *The Irish Times*, 25 August 2017.

5   W. Tigges, 'The Limerick: The Sonnet of Nonsense?' in W. Tigges (ed.), *Explorations in the Field of Nonsense* (Amsterdam: Rodopi, 1987), p. 117. See the other essays in this collection for further discussion, especially those by Lisa Ede, Hendrik van Leeuwen, and Elizabeth Sewell.

6   E. Lear, *So Much Nonsense*, intro. Q. Blake (Oxford: Bodleian Library, 2007), n.p.

7   N. Douglas, *Some Limericks* (London: Atlas Press, 2009), p. 70. Originally published 1928. Gershon Legman gives this as no. 116 in his *The Limerick: 1700 Examples, with Notes, Variants and Index* (New York: Bell, 1964), and dated 1927–1932.

8   B. Cerf, *Out On A Limerick*, illustrated by Saxon (New York: Harper & Row, 1987), p. 68. Originally published in 1960. Cerf's blurb promises 'A classic collection of more than 300 of the world's best printable limericks. Assembled, revised, dry-cleaned, and annotated by Bennet Cerf.'

9   For a determining modernist meditation on the subject of catalexis in doggerel, see Stephen Dedalus's thoughts in the Proteus episode of *Ulysses*: 'Am I walking into eternity along Sandymount strand? Crush, crack, crick, crick. Wild sea money. Dominie Deasy kens them a'. *Wont' you come to Sandymount, / Madeline the mare?* Rhythm begins, you see. I hear. Acatalectic tetrameter of iambs marching. No, agallop: *deline the mare*', James Joyce, *Ulysses: the corrected text* (London: Penguin, 1986), p. 31. Note that this must be one of the errors of the so-called 'corrected text': Stephen is discussing a clear instance of catalexis (the dropped unstressed portion of the first foot of each line), not the 'acatalectic'! We also find in the Aeolus section of the book 'LENEHAN'S LIMERICK': '*There's a ponderous pundit MacHugh / Who wears goggles of ebony hue. / As he mostly sees double / To wear them why trouble? I can't see the Joe Miller. Can you?*', p. 110. There is also Joyce's famous anathema against the Consul-General Percy Bennett: 'There's

an anthropoid consul called Bennett, / With the jowl of a jackass or jennet, / He must muzzle or mask it / In the waste paper basket, / When he rises to bray in the Senate.' Richard Ellmann has catalogued Joyce's enthusiasm for limericks, which run as a strange sequence of remarks and footnotes throughout the biography. These include: 'There was a kind priest called Delany / Who said to the girls, "Nota Bene, / 'Twould tempt the Archbishop / The way that you switch up / Your skirts when the weather is rainy', p. 88n. Also: 'There was a kind lady called Gregory, / Said "Come to me, poets in beggary," / But found her imprudence / When thousands of students / Cried, "All, we are in that category." p. 107n. Here is one on W. K. Magee, who wrote under the pseudonym of John Eglinton, and appears in the Scylla and Charybdis section of *Ulysses*: 'There once was a Celtic librarian / Whose essays were voted Spencerian, / His name is Magee / But it seems that to me / He's a flavour that's more Presbyterian.' p. 118n. A double limerick about the Fay brothers, p. 161, a friend Sykes, p. 394, about Victor Sax and the Austro-Hungarian Emperor, about Stephen, a donor, about H.G. Wells (only three lines survive), p. 414n, etc. There's also the famous response to Beckett's *Murphy*: 'There's a meavusmarked maggot called Murphy. / Who would fain be thought thunder-and-turfy. / When he's out to be chic he / Sticks on his gum dicky / And worms off for a breeze by the surfy', p. 701. Christopher Acklerley has also produced a sequence of 18 limericks retelling *Ulysses* which, to my chagrin, I have as yet been unable to acquire.

10   Bibby, p. 71.
11   See the examples provided by W.S. Baring-Gould, *The Lure of the Limerick: An Uninhibited History* (London: Rupert Hart-Davis, 1968), e.g., pp. 76–77.
12   Douglas, *Some Limericks*, p. 18.
13   Cited in Baring-Gould, p. 16.
14   I owe this observation to the work of Anna Cordner.

15 See, for example, G. Legman, *The Limerick: 1700 Examples, with Notes, Variants and Index* (London: Jupiter Books, 1974).

16 See G. Deleuze, *The Logic of Sense*, trans. M. Lester with C. Stivale (New York: Columbia University Press, 1990).

17 G. Legman (ed.), *The New Limerick, Second Series* (New York: Crown, 1977), p. ix. He at once goes on: 'A few disorganized females have been found in recent years, however, willing to match the standard cruel and castratory anti-woman limericks with equally cruel and castratory anti-man limericks of their own concocting.'

18 J. Lacan, *Formations of the Unconscious*, trans. R. Grigg (Cambridge: Polity, 2017), p. 102.

19 Bibby, p. 177.

20 It would then be no wonder if the limerick is also marked by the imperial absorption and suppression of colonised languages at its origin. See the extended self-published boutade of Críostóir Ó Floinn, *The Irish Origins of the 'Limerick'* (2018), which insists on the priority of the Maigue poets in its invention.

21 Legman, *The Limerick*, p. xli. Legman's own genealogy of the limerick runs from the Anglo-Saxon through the Elizabethan and Jacobean to the Georgian, with more or less plausibility if with a certain tendentiousness.

22 See R. Dawkins, *The Selfish Gene*, 30th anniversary edition (Oxford: Oxford University Press, 2006), esp. 'Chapter 11. Memes: The New Replicators', pp. 189–201.

23 John Maynard Smith, 'Genes and Memes', *London Review of Books*, Vol. 4, No. 2 (4 February 1982). As Smith continues: 'He would now, I think rightly, prefer to use the word "meme" only for the physical structure in the brain which represents the limerick. The spoken limerick is then the "phenotypic expression" of the meme—to a geneticist, the appearance and characteristics of an organism are its

"phenotype" as opposed to its "genotype", or genetic constitution. A meme can replicate, because if I, knowing a limerick, speak it aloud, the consequence is the appearance in your brain of a corresponding meme.'

24   Legman, *The New Limerick*, p. ix.

Biographical Notes

STÉPHANE MALLARMÉ (French, 1842–1898).
English teacher. Famed for snobbishness and
salons. Author of many refined verses. Against
vulgar uses of language, which he compared to
a worn coin passed silently from hand to hand.
Such aristocratic metaphors did not, however,
negate his petit-bourgeois enthusiasm for
money. As Robert Boncado has pointed out,
however, this limerick's claims 'might be belied
though by Mallarmé's expert wrangling of a
generous pension—awarded for early retire-
ment too'.

PLATO (Greek, c. 428/424–348 BC). Philosopher.
Plato was not his real name, but, according to
Diogenes Laertius, a moniker given to the boy
by his wrestling coach on account of his physical robustness. Plato had wanted to be a poet,
but, finding he was hopeless, invented philosophy out of rage at his own incompetence.
Phaedo is the name of the protagonist of one of
Plato's dialogues regarding the immortality of
the soul.

SOCRATES (Greek, c. 470–399 BC). Philosopher.
Supremely ugly with an unendurable personal-
ity, he was executed by the Athenians for
impiety and corrupting youth. Good riddance
to bad rubbish I say.

ST THOMAS AQUINAS (Italian, 1225–1274).
Dominican friar and Doctor of the Church.
Much like Plato, a famously large fellow.
The alleged limerick is as follows:

> *Sit vitiorum meorum evacuatio*
> *Concupiscentae et libidinis exterminatio,*
> *Caritatis et patientiae,*
> *Humilitatis et obedientiae,*
> *Omniumque virtutum augmentatio.*

The remarkable Ronald Knox is sometimes
alleged to be the first to identify this composition as indeed a forerunner of the limerick.
Two incomparable limericks, often assigned to
Knox himself, and which riff on the bizarre
idealist metaphysics of Bishop Berkeley, read
thus:

> There was a young man who said 'God
> Must find it exceedingly odd
> To think that the tree
> Should continue to be
> When there's no one about in the quad.'

Reply:

> 'Dear Sir: Your astonishment's odd;
> I am always about in the quad.
> And that's why the tree
> Will continue to be
> Since observed by, Yours faithfully, God.'

LAOZI (6th–4th century BC). Sage. Founder of philosophical Taoism. Conceived when his mother glimpsed a falling star. Laozi gestated for 62 years, before being born an old man. 'The Way', he says, 'The Way that can be spoken of, is not an unchanging Way.'

EMILY DICKINSON (American, 1830–1886). Supreme visionary poet. What a puritan! Preferred white clothing and intense verse.

BENEDICT SPINOZA (Dutch, 1632–1677). Atheist Jew of Voorburg. Lens-grinder. Expelled from the Jewish community of Amsterdam. His great treatise, the *Ethics*, contains the heretical assertion *Deus sive Natura*, that is, *God or Nature*. For Spinoza, God is not a creator of the world from outside—but the world itself.

MICHEL FOUCAULT (French, 1926–1984). Bald, bespectacled queer archivist. Notorious for books on the history of madness, prisons, sexuality, and knowledge. Conclusively demonstrates that claims to personal identity are not the royal road to liberation, but an insidious form of subjection to power. Ugh.

MARY SHELLEY (English, 1797–1851). Writer. Daughter of Mary Wollstonecraft and William Godwin. Married to Percy Bysshe Shelley. Author of *Frankenstein* and *The Last Man*. Mary is a veritable buccinator of apocalyptic posthuman thinking.

SIGMUND FREUD (Austrian, 1856–1939). Psychoanalyst. Tell me about your mother. No, please don't.

DIOGENES THE CYNIC (Greek, c. 403–323 BC). Dog. Ostracised with his father for debasing the coinage of Sinope. Fled to Athens to become a high-grade source of hippy anecdotage. Doggo lived in a barrel, mocked Plato and Alexander the Great, and masturbated in public. When upbraided for doing so, he replied: if only I could fix my hunger by rubbing my belly the same way. Get out of my fucking light you fucking bozos.

SIR FRANCIS BACON (English, 1561–1626). Corrupt essayist. Also: The Real Shakespeare and Authore of various werkes of naturall philosophie, nott to the execlosion of *Novum Organum* and *New Atlantis*. Very much liked the word 'new'. One-time Lord Chancellor of England, cashiered for corruption. Died after catching a cold buying a chicken from an old lady for experiments, thereby inventing the lethal *bacon parmigiana*. Who hasn't had one of those at an Aussie pub? Please note that, according to the immutable rituals of aristocratic etiquette, Franky should not properly be referred to as 'Lord Bacon'; his actual titles included 'Baron Verulam' in 1618 and, later, 'Viscount St. Alban' in 1621. Apparently a very distant forefather of the Irish painter of the same sham pain.

SAMUEL BECKETT (Irish, 1906–1989). Writer. Son of a quantity surveyor and a nurse, friend of James Joyce, and chauffeur to André the Giant. Immortalised in *Wisden Cricketers' Almanack*.

JEREMY BENTHAM (English, 1748–1832). Lawyer. Founder of utilitarianism, purveyor of a doctrine of fictional entities and developer of the controversial Panopticon; stuffed and dressed, now lives dead in a glassy cabinet in London.

RENÉ DESCARTES (French, 1596–1650). Philosopher and mathematician. Doubter, dualist, duellist, demonist. Invented the game *Battleships*. Killed by having to get up early.

LADY MURASAKI SHIKIBU (Japanese, c. 973–1014). Lady-in-Waiting at the Imperial Court of Japan. Author of *The Tale of Genji*. Her name is a pseudonym: it seems that nobody actually knows who she was.

JANE AUSTEN (English, 1775–1817). Author. Acid and forthright. Recognised that the problem of individuation is best exemplified by the life-changing decision, and there is no starker image of such a decision than impoverished middle-class teenage girls desperate to marry an aristocrat.

ZENO OF ELEA (Greek, c. 490–430 BC). Philosopher. Friend of Parmenides, inventor of the dialectic, constructor of paradoxes of movement. Will Achilles catch the tortoise? Will the arrow fly? Will you ever reach the end of this limerick?

OMAR KHAYYAM (Persian, 1048–1131). Mathematician and poet. Bertrand Russell in *The History of Western Philosophy* comments 'The only man known to me who was both a poet and a mathematician'. Khayyam seems to have been a heterodox, even atheist Muslim; a disciple of the founder of the Assassins; an agent of the state reform of the calendar (more accurate than the Gregorian); the author of texts on jewellery, the causes of climactic differences, algebra, Euclid, ontology and obligation. Taken together, his works show Omar to be practically engaged at the centre of the philosophy, art, science and politics of his time. That's crazy, right?

ALBERT CAMUS (French-Algerian, 1913–1960). Goalie, chain-smoker, writer, absurdist.

CONFUCIUS (Chinese, 551–479 BC). Traditionalist, moralist, loyalist. Ancestrally-oriented. Winner of the Hundred Schools of Thought tournament. Study first—talk later!

AIMÉ CÉSAIRE (Martinican, 1913–2008). Poet and politician. A founder of the *négritude* movement and author of *Cahier d'un retour au pays natal*. Now has an airport named after him.

SIMONE DE BEAUVOIR (French, 1908–1986). Feminist existentialist activist. Author of *Le deuxième sexe*, which contains the immortal lines 'One is not born, but becomes a woman'.

SIMONE WEIL (French, 1909–1943). Pacifist, anarchist, mystic. Enjoyed several episodes of religious ecstasy founded on her *scintilla synderesis*. 'Every event that takes place', she writes, 'is a syllable pronounced by the voice of Love'. Ho-hum.

ÉVARISTE GALOIS (French, 1811–1832). Teen prodigy. A fervent republican, founded mathematical group theory and methods that enabled him to determine for any polynomial equation whether it has a solution by radicals. Shot in the stomach in a duel over a woman, abandoned by his friends, slung in a common grave.

KARL MARX (German, 1818–1883). Revolutionary. Former Young Hegelian, journalist, materialist theorist of exploitation, of the labour theory of value, of constitutive social antagonism, of alienation under capitalism, and the functioning of commodity fetishism. Notorious panhandler and drunk.

JOHN MILTON (English, 1608–1674). Puritan, republican, poet. Supporter of the English Revolution, Secretary to Oliver Cromwell, author of many fine texts justifying the execution of monarchs, as well as several alright poems. A fine organist.

ALEXANDER GROTHENDIECK (German-French-stateless, 1928–2014). Mathematician and keeper of sheep. As a teenager, his parents in internment or concentration camps, he was often in hiding. Father murdered at Auschwitz. Refused to sign a form promising he wouldn't work to overthrow the USA. An anecdote tells us that, while studying, his supervisor gave him a list of crucial currently-unsolved mathematical problems from which he should choose one or two to which to dedicate his life; young Alex returned a few months later, having solved the lot. Dandelion soup for all!

FRANTZ FANON (Martinican, 1925–1961). Psychiatrist and revolutionary. Author of *Black Skin, White Masks* and *The Wretched of the Earth*. Decolonisation will be violent, or it will not be.

GEORG CANTOR (German, 1845–1918). Mathematician. Inventor of set theory. Proved that the size or cardinality of the infinity of the natural numbers is smaller than the cardinality of the infinity of the real numbers, a result he claimed was given him by God. Despite the infuriated rejection of Cantor's demonstrations by the greatest mathematicians—which, some say, led to the former's recurrent bouts of severe depression, for which he was frequently institutionalised—David Hilbert declared

'We shall not be expelled from Cantor's Paradise!'

GEORGES BATAILLE (French, 1897–1962). Oddball numismatic son of a syphilitic tax collector. Ejected from the Surrealists for a too-hearty enjoyment of Salvador Dali's scato-logical images. Who can say whether the physicochemical world is in pain or not? A storm is the world jerking off! Come as you aren't!

YUKIO MISHIMA (Japanese, 1925–1970). Reactionary bodybuilder and actor. His father, a government official, detested Mishima being involved in the effeminate craft of literary writing. His grandmother did not allow Mishima into the sunlight. Lover of the writings of Georges Bataille. Founded his own ultra-right-wing militia on the basis that the Emperor should never have caved to Western pressure in WWII by announcing that he was not a god. Attempted a coup, then suicide. Mishima's decapitation was botched by his designated second. So intense.

JOHN KEATS (English, 1795–1821). Doctor and author. Totally tubercular. His inheritance was stripped from him unjustly. No wonder he was obsessed with the false gold of poetry. W. B. Yeats said he was like a little boy with his nose pressed to a sweet-shop window.

HANNAH ARENDT (German, 1906–1975).
Political thinker. A famous beauty in her youth,
the assimilated Jew Arendt enjoyed a notorious
affair with her (soon-to-be-Nazi) teacher,
the philosopher Martin Heidegger. After
WWII, Arendt became a citizen of the USA.
W. H. Auden was a close friend and once pro-
posed marriage. Though she never had children
herself, Arendt nominated 'natality' as *the*
fundamental political category. In later years,
Diana Trilling remarked that Arendt kept her
husband tied to the bed 'for use when necessary'.

WALLACE STEVENS (American, 1879–1955).
Lawyer and insurance officer, son of another
lawyer. Lutheran. Full of fun. Hardly left
Hartford Accident and Indemnity Company
after 1916, except to go to Key West, Florida, to
get drunk and abuse writers. Once literally
smacked into a 'fresh rain-water puddle' by
Ernest Hemingway, with whom he had fool-
ishly picked a fight. Was informed by Robert
Frost that his poems were 'too executive'.
A Boyar was a member of the old Russian
aristocracy.

SØREN KIERKEGAARD (Danish, 1813–1855).
Lutheran. Notoriously witty. For instance: if
every true Christian should be a contemporary
of Christ, what did Christ's actual contempo-
raries think of him? They disbelieved in his
divinity. How, then, to be true believers in
Christ? We must doubt his divinity. So: true

belief without true doubt impossible. Wrote books under a plethora of parodic pseudonyms. What a guy.

KARL POPPER (Austrian-British, 1902–1994). Philosopher of science and political theorist. Refused entry by Australia, moved to New Zealand during WWII, emigrated to Britain in 1946. Created the demarcation criterion of 'falsifiability', i.e., a scientific proposition is true iff it is synthetic (i.e., its negation is not a contradiction) and there is as yet no attested or reproducible instance of an empirical phenomenon or event that contradicts it. In other words: if you are indeed true, you are permanently on notice that you may not be. What other form of knowledge offers that? Nothing. Please spare me your opinion.

JUNICHIRO TANIZAKI (Japanese, 1886–1965). Reactionary writer and snob. Author of many excellent writings. In *In Praise of Shadows* he condemns the introduction of electricity for destroying the Japanese kingdom of shadows.

JORGE LUIS BORGES (Argentinian, 1899–1986). Poet, editor and essayist. One of the most erudite persons of the 20th century. A friend who studied Shakespeare with Borges in Buenos Aires in the late 1950s tells me that, already blind, he would be led into class by a beautiful young woman or two, whereupon, off the top of his head, he would deliver a word-perfect lecture on one or another Shakespeare play for two hours. Clearly a memorious gentleman, like God or Funes, or someone like that.

VIRGINIA WOOLF (English, 1882–1941). Ruling-class English writer and doyenne of Bloomsbury. With her husband Leonard, founded the Hogarth Press. In the essay *A Room of One's Own*, she famously declares 'Give her a room of her own and five hundred a year'. Rooms and guineas for all, not just the rich!

OODGEROO NOONUCCAL (Australian, 1920–1993). Activist and author. First Aboriginal Australian to publish a book of poetry, *We Are Going* (1964). As her later biographies read: 'Most Australians know her as Kath Walker, the name she was given by white people, but in 1988 she decided to change her name to identify more closely with her Aboriginal heritage.' 'Oodgeroo' means 'paperbark' in Nunukal.

NED KELLY (Australian, 1854–1880). Bullet-proof bushranger. Declared an outlaw twice by Queen Victoria. Dictated the outrageous *Jerilderie Letter* to his mate Joe Byrne. Last words: 'Such is life'. There is a tale that his testicles were turned into a tobacco pouch by a jailor. Smoke 'em if you got 'em.

GEORGE ELIOT (English, 1819–1880). Author. Real name: Mary Anne Evans. Translated

Spinoza's *Ethics* and denied the Christian faith. Boo! Lived openly with George Henry Lewes, who was married to Agnes Jervis, with whom he had three children. Jervis had also had children by Thornton Leigh Hunt, whose names had appeared on the birth certificate as Lewes's. Sadly, this made him technically complicit in the adultery, and prevented his divorce from Jervis.

JOHN DONNE (English, 1572–1631). Poet and priest. Abjured the Catholic faith into which he had been born. Married Anne More in 1601, against parental and employer wishes. Fired and arrested. Sent letter to Anne: *John Donne, Anne Donne, Un-done.* Lots of children but no money. One child is dying, he wrote, which is good because there will be one less mouth to feed; but not so good because we can't afford to bury him. Hard times. Later lectured Charles I on Nothing. Wrote a little tract on suicide titled *Biathanatos*, much admired by Borges.

H.D. (American, 1886–1961). Poet. Full name: Hilda Doolittle. Friends with Ezra Pound and Sigmund Freud. With the former and Richard Aldington, invented Imagism. Later wrote books such as *Trilogy* and *Helen in Egypt*.

VAL PLUMWOOD (Australian, 1939–2008). Philosopher. Born: Val Morell. Changed surname to 'Plumwood' after divorcing from her husband David Routley, a philosopher and

logician, who later changed his own surname to
'Sylvan'. In 1985 she was attacked by a crocodile
in Kakadu National Park. Her thoughts on *being
prey* stemmed from this event.

FRANÇOIS VILLON (French, 1431 – c. 1463).
Criminal and poet. Raised by his uncle
Guillaume de Villon, whose name he took;
other documents list Montcorbier and Loges.
A member of various criminal gangs, Villon
ended up being tortured by both church and
state, and his accomplices executed. 'Mouton'
was a fake name he gave once on being arrested
for stabbing a priest in the groin. Author of one
of the greatest works of poetry of all time:
Le Grand Testament. Where *are* the snows of
yesteryear?!

ZORA NEALE HURSTON (American, 1891–1960).
African-American anthropologist and author.
Wrote accounts of slave ships, and gathered
folktales. Also wrote the extraordinary personal
testimony 'How It Feels to Be Colored Me', and
the realist novel *Their Eyes Were Watching God*.

GIACOMO TALDEGARDO FRANCESCO DI SALES
SAVERIO PIETRO LEOPARDI (Italian, 1798–1837).
Try writing that in triplicate. Aristocratic
philologist and poet. Depressive and sickly.
Author of *L'infinito*. Oh, it was all hills and
hedges, ills and sledges with little Giacomo.

PARMENIDES (Greek, fl. sixth–fifth century BC).

Philosopher-Poet. Founder of the Eleatic School, which included the aforementioned Zeno. All that remains of his great poem are fragments. What it is thought it presents is: one being, everlasting, unchanging; for something to be many is not to be one; to not be one is not to be anything; to not be anything is not to be; but not-being is impossible, so there must be being; being must be one. Etc.

DU FU (Chinese, 712–770). Poet and thwarted bureaucrat. Through bad luck, Du Fu lived in turbulent times. The An Lushan rebellion displaced or killed 35 million or so people. Cripes. His administrative ambitions suffered, but the experience seems to have helped his poetry.

MARY WOLLSTONECRAFT (English, 1759–1797). Feminist author. Mother of Mary Shelley. Turbulent relationships with Henry Fuseli and Gilbert Imlay, before taking up with William Godwin. William Blake illustrated several of her early works. Author of *A Vindication of the Rights of Men*, following it with *A Vindication of the Rights of Woman*.

CHRISTINA ROSSETTI (English, 1830–1894). Poet. Daughter of Gabriele Rossetti and Frances Polidori, whose brother was Byron's physician, and who was there on the famous night that the Shelleys and Byron decided to try their hand at a gothic story. Polidori's attempt,

The Vampyre, is the first modern short story containing that eponymous creature. Christina's own brothers Dante and William were the founders of the Pre-Raphaelite Brotherhood. Christina herself seems to have been a kind of child prodigy. Her most famous poem remains 'Goblin Market'. Don't eat the sticky fruits children.

NAGARJUNA (Indian, c. 150 – c. 250). Hindu convert to Buddhism. Sometimes known as 'the second Buddha'. Realised that *sunyata* —from *sunya*, the instability of existence, the number zero—must be the non-central-centre of being-as-becoming. Nagarjuna is a kind of anti-Parmenides, who thought only of the eternal One. For Nagarjuna reasoned: without inexistence, no instability; without instability, no change; without change, no being. Died cutting off his own head with a leaf of grass.

ST PAUL (Tarsan, c. 5 – c. 64). Tentmaker.

GUSTAVE FLAUBERT (French, 1821–1880). Writer. Snob. Author of *Madame Bovary*, which was called before the courts for immorality. The limerick alludes to the famous lines from *Bovary*: 'human language is like a cracked kettle on which we beat out tunes for bears to dance to, when what we long to do is make music that will move the stars to pity'. Yeah, yeah, we are all in the gutters, etc., etc.

GWEN HARWOOD (Australian, 1920–1995). Poet and housewife. In 1961 she submitted a couple of sonnets entitled 'Eloisa to Abelard' and 'Abelard to Eloisa' to the magazine *The Bulletin* under the pseudonym Walter Lehmann. Only after publication did the editors—one of whom was the eminent Donald Horne—realise that the first letter of each line vertically spelled out: *So lOng bULLetIN* and *Fuck AlL eDiToRs*.

URSULA K. LE GUIN (American, 1929–2018). Fantasy writer. In the *Earthsea* series, Le Guin writes of the hero Ged as unleashing through his own actions a formless darkness from within that will pursue him for ever.

WILLIAM BLAKE (English, 1757–1827). Writer and illustrator. What a crank!

MELANIE KLEIN (Austrian-English, 1882–1960). Child psychiatrist. Developer of object relations theory. Moved to London in 1926. Saw a lot of paranoid-schizoid savagery in the fantasies of little children. Klein was herself famously antipathetic and argumentative.

G.W.F. HEGEL (German, 1770–1831). Philosopher. Absolute idealist. *O how much dough there is in the German spirit! Ich bin ein Berliner!*

JUDITH WRIGHT (Australian, 1915–2000). Poet and environmentalist.

GERSHON LEGMAN (American, 1917–1999).
Folklorist. Son of a kosher Hungarian butcher.
Legman must have been an infamy from
infancy. Jay Landesman in the *Independent*
mentions that at school 'his fellow classmates
wrote the word "kosher" in horseshit juice
across his forehead. It left a deep impression.'
I'll bet. Collector, purveyor and producer of
erotica and other sub-literary fictions, includ-
ing a short-story titled *The Poisoned Enema*,
Legman was perfectly aware of the import and
irony of his assumed name. In addition to
doing some work for Kinsey, Legman claims to
have invented the 'vibrating dildo', an invention allegedly stolen by one Dr. Vladimir
Fortunato, a 'famous anatomical model-maker'
who also claimed to be the first man to have
undergone a vasectomy. Legman was also an
aficionado of origami, and one of the most
dynamic and influential disseminators of the
art in the West. He also claims to have coined
the phrase 'Make Love Not War'. Finally, in
addition to these (and many other) extraordinary acts, Legman is—despite his professed
distaste for the form—one of the greatest
anthologists of the limerick.

W.B. YEATS (Irish, 1865–1939). Poet. Big fan of
ghost stories, cranks, quacks, mountebanks,
frauds, clowns, fascists and words like 'maiden'.
Obsessed with Maud Gonne. Lots of early
poems about Celtic myths and Irish folklore.
Great stuff.

OSCAR WILDE (Irish, 1854–1900). Celebrity and wit. Accused by the Marquess of Queensberry of 'posing somdomite', after suspecting Wilde's relationship with the Marquess's son, Lord Alfred Douglas or 'Bosie'. Wilde sued for libel.

CLARICE LISPECTOR (Brazilian, 1920–1977). Writer. Lispector's Ukrainian Jewish family fled Podolia to Brazil while she was still an infant. Began to write stream-of-consciousness monologues focussing on intense internal states. Rest, history.

EMMY NOETHER (German, 1882–1935). Mathematician. Rings, fields, symmetries, that's what it's about. David Hilbert and Felix Klein invited her to teach at Göttingen, where she stayed until the Nazis banned her from further teaching because of her Jewish heritage. Moved to the United States, died.

THOMAS DE QUINCEY (English, 1785–1859). Hack writer, alcoholic, and opium addict. Permanently on the run from his creditors. Exceedingly short, de Quincey was allegedly the only person able to stand fully erect in Dove Cottage, celebrated home of Will and Dot Wordsworth for the first years of the 19th century. De Quincey is perhaps most famous as the author of the first great drug-memoir of modern times, *Confessions of an English Opium Eater*.

IMMANUEL KANT (German, 1724–1804). Philosopher. Loved Königsberg. So regular in his habits, the housewives of Königsberg allegedly used to set their clocks by him. According to legend, missed his walk only twice in his life: first, when he was reading Rousseau; second, when he heard of the French Revolution. Bring me my snappy garters at once John!

PYTHAGORAS (Greek, c. 570 – c. 495 BC). Cult leader. Golden-thighed bean-hating magic-worker. May have invented the words *mathematics* and *philosophy*. His supposed 'Theorem' concerning the squares of the sides of right-angled triangle had been known for at least 1000 years prior to his birth by the Babylonians and the Indians. The incident in question in this limerick concerns the irrationality of the square root of two, which contravenes the Pythagorean dictum that the universe is a matter of ratios: Hippasus, who supposedly told the world the secret, was drowned by the cult for his troubles.

HYPATIA (Alexandrian, c. 350–415). Mathematician and philosopher. Murdered by a mob of Christian monks armed with sea-shells, or, alternatively, roof tiles.

ERICH AUERBACH (German, 1892–1957). Philologist and critic. Of Jewish heritage, Auerbach was forced to leave his job by the

Nazis. He moved to Istanbul, where he wrote his masterwork, *Mimesis*. He himself says that he would never have written such a book if he had had all his familiar library about him. When he moved to the US after the war, his students were so struck by his creepy *Mitteleuropean* manner and accent that he became the model for Nosferatu in B-grade American horror movies. Philology is vampirism.

HERACLITUS (Greek, c. 535 – c. 475 BC). Philosopher. Very obscure. Celebrated misanthrope. One of the stories of Heraclitus's death is that, suffering from dropsy, he rolled in cow shit in the expectation that the warm excrement would dry out his swollen humours. Good luck with that one, mate.

MARCEL PROUST (French, 1871–1922). Writer. Man of fashion. Social climber.

MINA LOY (English, 1882–1966). Poet and painter. Hung out in Paris with Gertrude Stein and friends. Married, children. Met Marinetti. Dumped them all and moved to New York. Hung out in New York with Marcel Duchamp and Marianne Moore. Had an affair with Arthur Cravan, who disappeared off the coast of Mexico. Went here and there. Died in Aspen.

MARGUERITE DURAS (French, 1914–1996). Writer. Born Marguerite Donnadieu in French

Indochina, where, as a teenager, she had an affair with an older Chinese man, now severally immortalised in her various autobiographies of the events. Married for a time to Robert Antelme, who was incarcerated in Dachau; after she'd nursed him back to health on his return, she dumped him for his friend Dionys Mascolo. Wrote the script for *Hiroshima Mon Amour*.

MARIANNE MOORE (American, 1887–1972). Writer. Never met her father, who'd had a psychotic break and had been institutionalised before her birth. Co-dependent with her mother, Mary; William Carlos Williams referred to it as her 'mother thing'. Edited *The Dial*, an important little magazine. As she wrote in a note: 'Omissions are not accidents—M.M.'

Limericks, Philosophical & Literary
Justin Clemens

Design: Brad Haylock

First edition 2019
ISBN: 978-1-922099-36-5
Edition of 300

Surpllus
PO Box 418
Flinders Lane 8009
Victoria, Australia

www.surpllus.com

Surpllus respectfully acknowledges the people of the Woi wurrung and Boon wurrung language groups of the eastern Kulin nations as the traditional owners of the unceded lands upon which the development of this book has principally taken place.

Justin Clemens teaches at The University of Melbourne. His books include *Minimal Domination*, also published by Surpllus.

We gratefully acknowledge the School of Culture and Communication at The University of Melbourne for its support of this publication.

Surpllus #30